English

The Language of Love

For it was not into my ear you whispered, but into my heart
'Twas not my lips you kissed, but my soul
Judy Garland

About the book

*Falling in love is easy
if you meet the right person...*

*But what if Mr or Ms Right
doesn't speak your language?*

*From asking someone out and going on a date
To falling in love, romance and more*

*This book gives you
all the English you need to speak
the Language of Love*

Copyright

Published by The Whole World Company, Cambridge, England

Paperback edition (1.0) © The Whole World Company Limited 2016

Printed by CreateSpace

ISBN 978-1-903384-07-7

About us

The Whole World Company donates a small portion of profits
to children's education, health and welfare
in poorer countries of the world.

If you have any suggestions for the *Language of Love*,
for your language or culture,
visit www.whole-world.co/love

To my darlings J and S

If you live to be a hundred
I want to live to be a hundred minus one day
So I never have to live without you
Winnie the Pooh

Contents

Contents

Meeting Mr or Ms Right

Mr or Ms Right means the man or woman who's just right for you – the one you will marry

Close to you

Excuse me. May I sit next to you?

Hello

I'm *Name*

Where are you from?

I'm from *Country*

Have we met before?
I think I've seen you at *place*

Love isn't something you find
Love is something that finds you
Loretta Young, actress

Help

Are you OK? Can I help you?

Do you need some help?

Excuse me. Could you help me?

Lost and found

Are you lost?

I'm looking for the *Art Gallery*. Could you show me how to get there?

Can you give me directions?
Where to?
Your heart

Small talk

It's a beautiful day, isn't it

I love the winter/spring/summer/autumn or fall

If it's raining...
Would you like to share my umbrella?

At a café

Do you know a *café* or *restaurant* nearby?

Excuse me. May I share a table with you?

I'm sorry, but I can't understand the menu. Could you help me?

What would you recommend?

Travel

On a bus, train, boat or plane...
Excuse me. May I sit next to you?

Are you going to *London*?

Do you like *New York*?

I'm on holiday/vacation
I work here

I just got here

I'm staying for *three* days/weeks/months

What should I see in *Sydney*?

Do you know any good places to go?

Reading

What are you reading?

Can you recommend a book about *New Zealand*?

Music

What are you listening to?

About a song playing
I love this song
Do you know the name of this song/singer/band?

What kind of music do you like?

Do you like *jazz*?

At a club or bar

Would you like to dance?

I'm not a good dancer

You're a great dancer

Compliments

I like your ___
— tie
— dress
— hair
— style

You have a lovely smile
You have beautiful eyes

I'm very happy we met

love
letters
only

Traditions of love: Happiness starts with U

In America, young women used to pare an apple and throw the peel over their shoulder. The shape of the fallen peel would spell the first letter of her future husband's name.

Asking someone out

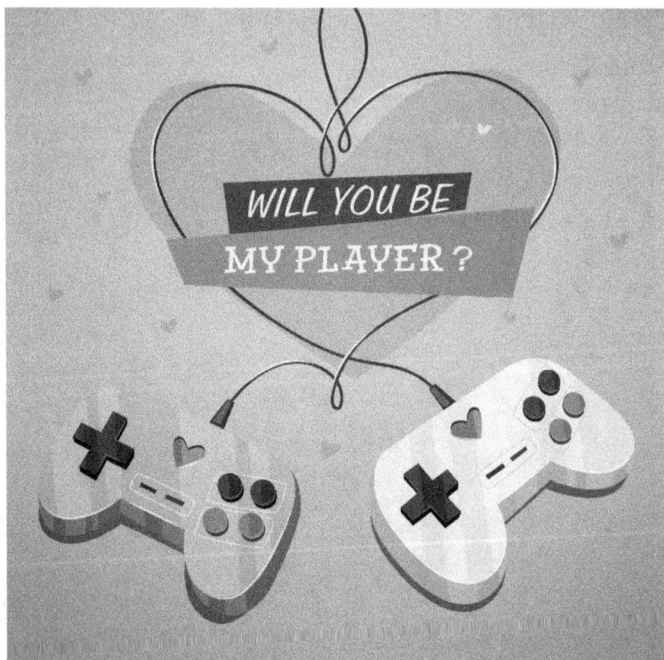

WILL YOU BE MY PLAYER ?

I'm really nervous

I feel really awkward
= *you feel nervous and clumsy*

I've got butterflies in my stomach
= *butterflies means you have a fluttering, nervous feeling inside*

Would you like to...?

Would you like to *get a coffee*?

Would you like to *have lunch*?

My friends are *having dinner/a party/a barbecue*, would you like to join us?

Something in the way she moves
attracts me like no other lover
The Beatles, *Something*

In touch

Can I call you?
— What's your phone number?

Can I text/email you?
— What's your number/email address?

Are you on *Facebook®*?

Time and place

Are you free *tomorrow*?
— Yes, I'm free all day
— I'm busy *tomorrow*, but I'm free on *Saturday*

How about *Sunday*?

What time shall we meet?
— Shall we meet at *7*?
— I'll pick you up at *8*

Where shall we meet?
— Shall we meet at *café*?
— Shall we meet in front of *Place*

If you're busy

I'm not sure

I'm busy that day

I'm sorry I can't

Traditions of love: Love plants and potions

In the southern USA, people traditionally plant vervain near the entrance to their house to attract a lover. And men and women everywhere wear cologne and perfume to do the same.

Going on a date

Wow!

You look ___
— beautiful ♀
— wonderful ♀
That's a beautiful *dress*

You look ___
— very handsome ♂
— very smart (= well-dressed)
I love your suit/shirt/tie ♂

Something to do

Would you like to ___?
— go for coffee
— have lunch
— have a picnic
— have dinner
— see a movie
— go to the theater
— go to an art gallery
— go to a concert
— go to the opera
— go to the ballet
— go dancing
— go to a club
— go for a walk
— go for a bike ride
— go for a drive
— go skating
— play tennis
— go to the zoo
— go to the beach
— go sailing
— go on a hot air balloon

Moving on

Shall we go somewhere else?
— Yes, it's still early
— No, it's already late
— No, I'm tired

Going home

Sorry, I have to go now

Would you like a lift home?

Shall I walk you home/to the *station*?

— No thanks, I'll take the train/the bus/a taxi

Please call/text/email me when arrive so I know you got home safely

When will I see you again?

I really enjoyed today/*this evening*

I had a wonderful time
— Me, too

Can I see you again?
— Yes, I'd like that *very much*

How about *tomorrow*?

I'll text you 'Goodnight'

Traditions of love: Posies

A posy is a small bunch of flowers. One traditional posy included cabbage roses, pansies, larkspur, honeysuckle, wallflowers, snapdragons, gorse, lavender and lad's love, tied with sweet briar and ribbon grass.

In olden days, a man would give a posy to the woman he desired. If she threw it down, she was not interested; but if she kept the posy, the couple would start dating.

Describing you

A rose by any other name would smell as sweet
Shakespeare

What you look like

I have ___ hair
— short
— shoulder-length
— long
— black/brown/♀ blonde/♂ fair/red/gray

I'm ___
— 20
— about 30
— in my twenties/thirties/forties
— a golden oldie (= not young but still full of life)

I'm ___
— slim
— cuddly (= you have a lovely round shape)
— ♀ petite (= small and delicate)
— quite tall

Personality

I'm ___
— affectionate
— down-to-earth (= practical and realistic)
— easy-going (= relaxed and tolerant)
— outgoing (= confident and like meeting people)
— passionate (= you have strong feelings)
— quiet
— romantic

— sensitive
— shy
— sporty (= you like playing sports)
— thoughtful
— untidy

My friends say I'm...

My friends say I'm ___
— adventurous (= you always want to try new experiences)
— ambitious
— artistic
— caring
— a chatterbox (= you love talking)
— always cheerful
— like a child
— competitive (= you want to win at everything)
— crazy
— completely disorganized
— emotional
— flirty
— funny
— generous
— hardworking
— honest
— very independent (= you don't depend on others' support)
— a good listener (= you listen to your friend's problems)
— loud
— loyal (= you always help your friends)

— a little naïve
— a one-off (= you're unique)
— very organized
— quiet
— quirky (= a little strange, in a nice way)
— a little serious
— strong-minded (= very determined)
— stubborn
— not very stylish
— very tidy
— tolerant
— warm (= kind and loving)

My friends say I have a sense of humor (= you like telling jokes)

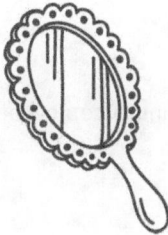

No-one's perfect

I'm sometimes a little ___
— arrogant (= you think you're better than others)
— big-headed
— bossy
— compulsive (= doing the same thing over and over again)

— cowardly
— cynical (= you see something bad even in good things)
— fussy (= you're too concerned about little details)
— grumpy
— gullible (= you're easily fooled)
— impatient
— impulsive (= you do things suddenly, without thinking)
— inconsiderate (= you don't think of others' feelings)
— indecisive (= you can't decide)
— intolerant
— jealous
— lazy
— materialistic (= money and possessions are very important to you)
— moody (= sometimes you're in a bad mood)
— narrow-minded
— obsessive
— overcritical
— possessive (= you want to control other people)
— quick-tempered
— rude
— selfish
— stingy (= you don't like spending money)
— stubborn
— timid (= you're shy and unadventurous)
— unreliable
— untidy

I'm not a perfect girl.
My hair doesn't always stay in place and I spill things a lot.
I'm pretty clumsy and sometimes I have a broken heart.
My friends and I sometimes fight and some days nothing goes right.
But when I think about it and take a step back
I remember how amazing life truly is
and that maybe, just maybe, I like being imperfect!
Anonymous

Getting to know each other

My favorite things

I like ___
I love ___
— art
— books
— Christmas
— the color of autumn leaves
— food
— my family and friends
— holidays
— music
— the outdoors (= you love nature and being outside)
— the smell after it's been raining
— the smell of freshly baked bread
— the sound of the ocean
— smiles
— sport
— sunshine
— taking a hot bath
— watching the sun set
— weekends

I don't like ___
I hate ___

— dishonest people
— getting up in the morning
— negative people
— rude people
— being single

What you do

What do you do?
— I'm a student
— I'm working

What are you studying?
— I'm studying *English*
— I'm studying to be a(n) ___

Where do you work?
— I work for *Company*

I'm a(n) ___
— architect
— artist
— cabin attendant
— designer
— doctor
— engineer
— journalist
— lawyer
— musician
— nurse

— pilot
— social worker
— teacher
— vet
— writer

I think you are...

You have a lovely personality

I think you're really ___
— caring
— chatty (= you love talking)
— cheerful
— clever
— down-to-earth (= practical and realistic)
— exciting
— feminine
— flirty
— funny
— generous
— honest
— intelligent
— kind
— masculine
— outgoing (= confident and like meeting people)
— positive
— romantic
— sensitive

— sexy
— smart (= smart means either intelligent or well-dressed)
— strong-minded
— sweet
— talented
— thoughtful
— unique

*Did the sun come out
Or did you just smile?*

We are so alike!

They say opposites attract
= *two people who are very different complement each other*

We're made for each other
= *you're perfect for each other*

Q&A

I want to know all about you
— Ask me anything you like

What's your favorite ___?
— food
— pizza
— flavor of ice cream
— song
— book
— movie
— place in the world

Dreams

What's your dream for the future?

Who do you admire most in the world?

If you could wish for anything, what would you wish for?

I like someone who is...

What do you look for in a guy/girl/man/woman?

I like someone who is ___
— adventurous (= you always want to try new experiences)
— affectionate
— ambitious
— artistic
— caring
— confident
— considerate (= thinks of others, not just him or herself)
— down-to-earth (= practical and realistic)
— easy-going (= relaxed and tolerant)
— funny
— generous
— hardworking
— honest
— a good listener (= you listen to your friend's problems)
— loyal (= you always help your friends)
— outgoing (= confident and like meeting people)
— passionate (= has strong feelings)
— positive
— quiet
— quirky (= a little strange, in a nice way)
— romantic
— sensitive
— serious
— smart
— sporty

— thoughtful
— tolerant
— warm (= kind and loving)

I like someone with a sense of humor

What's the most important thing for you ___?
— in a friend
— in a relationship

How long will you stay *here*?

Getting personal

How old are you?
— How old do I look?

You must be very popular

I guess you have a boyfriend/girlfriend *already/back home*?

Are you married?
— I'm divorced

Do you have children?
— I have a boy/girl
— I have *two* children *from my previous marriage*
— My children are grown up

Traditions of love: Leaping the broomstick

Gypsy couples marry by 'leaping the broomstick' – jumping over a branch of broom – a shrub with sweet-scented yellow flowers. If the woman's skirt touches the broomstick, she's already expecting a baby; if the man's trousers touch it, he will be unfaithful.

Dinner for two

Would you like to have dinner?

I know a lovely restaurant in ___
The food is delicious
It has a wonderful view

Do you like ___?
Do you like *Country* food?

Love at first bite

This is really romantic

You look lovely ♀
You look very handsome ♂

What would you like to eat?

Would you like some *wine*?
— Yes, please
— No, thanks. Just a soft drink, please

This is delicious
It's divine
= *divine means it tastes heavenly*

Would you like dessert?

Would you like *some coffee*?
Do you take sugar?
— No, I'm sweet enough already

After dinner

I'll pay
— No, I'll pay
— No thanks. I'll pay for myself

Shall we split the bill? (= you pay half each)

This was a lovely dinner

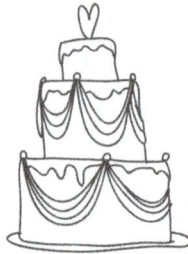

Traditions of love: Wedding cake

In Roman times, after a wedding ceremony a sweet cake of wheat or barley was broken over the bride's head. The bride and groom then ate some of the cake together, and the wedding guests gathered up the crumbs as tokens of good luck. When all the cakes were gone, guests were given handfuls of confetto – a mixture of nuts, dried fruit and honeyed almonds.

In medieval England, small spiced buns were stacked in a towering pile to make a wedding cake, as high as possible. If the bride and groom could kiss over the stack without knocking it over, they would enjoy a happy life.

In seventeenth-century Britain there were two wedding cakes, a hearty groom's cake, made of dried fruit, and a lighter bride-cake, decorated with sugar. Nowadays, the two cakes are often combined. In Britain wedding cakes today are nearly always made of dried fruit, like the earlier groom's cake, but are decorated with white sugar icing, like the bridecake. In America the groom's cake is given as a gift to guests to take home. It's called 'dreaming bread', because if you put a piece under your pillow, you'll dream of your future partner.

Today, the bride and groom cut the wedding cake together and feed each other the first slice in a ritual sharing of food, as in ancient Rome, symbolizing consummation of the marriage. Some of the wedding cake is kept for the blessing of the couple's first baby.

Lucky charms such as a coin or ring are sometimes hidden in the wedding cake. The person who gets the lucky slice will be blessed with fortune.

Apple pie without some cheese is
like a kiss without a squeeze
Proverb

Perfect day

I really enjoyed today
I had a wonderful time
— Me, too

It's been a perfect day

Would you like to do something *tomorrow*?

Shall I compare thee to a summer's day
Thou art more lovely and more temperate
Shakespeare, sonnet XX

Love at first sight

It had to be you
From the movie *Casablanca*

Love at first sight is when you fall in love with someone the first time you see them

I fell in love the moment I saw you

I didn't believe in love at first sight until I met you

When I first saw you, my heart skipped a beat
= *when you first saw him or her, your heart stopped*

I felt the chemistry between us straight away
= *chemistry is a special excitement and bond between two people*

Did my heart love till now?
Forswear it sight
For I ne'er saw true beauty
Till this night
Shakespeare, *Romeo and Juliet*

The first time I saw you, I knew you were the One
= *the One is the man or woman you're meant to be with for the rest of your life*

You are the love of my life
= *the person you will love forever*

Traditions of love: Cupid

Cupid is a winged cherub carrying a bow and a quiver of arrows. He is the Roman god of love, and whoever he shoots will fall in love.

Falling in love

You're the closest to heaven that I'll ever be
GooGoo Dolls

I think about you all the time

I can't get you out of my mind
= *whatever you do, you're always thinking of him or her*

I'm falling in love with you
= *when you start to love someone, you say 'falling in love'*

When you smile my heart skips a beat
= *when he or she smiles, your heart stops beating for a moment*

I'm captivated by you
= *you're are fascinated and enchanted by him or her*

*Gravitation is not responsible
for people falling in love*
Albert Einstein

I've got a crush on you
= *a strong attraction to someone, usually older than you*

You've stolen my heart
= *when you fall in love with someone, you say they have stolen your heart*

I've fallen in love with ___
— your smile
— your laugh
— you

I've fallen head over heels in love with you
= *you've fallen utterly and completely in love*

You've swept me off my feet ♂
= *if he sweeps you off your feet, you feel like you're are being carried on a wave of happiness*

You're perfect

Hold my hand

Hold me

Traditions of love: Venus and Aphrodite

Venus was the Roman goddess of love. Associated with love and feminine beauty, she has often been portrayed in art, such as Botticelli's Birth of Venus. The statue of the Greek goddess of love and beauty, Aphrodite, without arms, is known as Venus de Milo.

Fate (it's written in the stars)

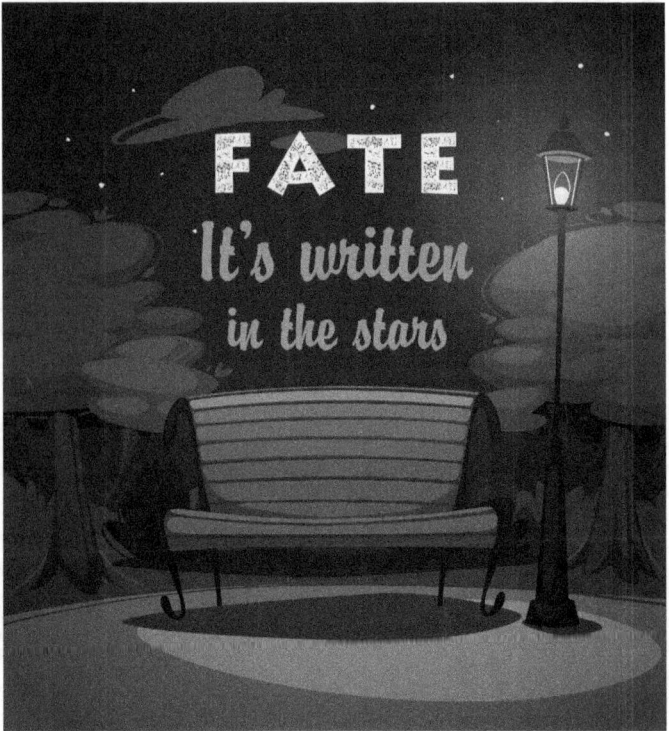

What star sign are you?

I'm ___
— Aries
— Taurus
— Gemini

— Cancer
— Leo
— Virgo
— Libra
— Scorpio
— Sagittarius
— Capricorn
— Aquarius
— Pisces

It's fate that we met

It's written in the stars
= *being together is your destiny*

If my plane/boat/train/bus had not been delayed, we never would have met

If I hadn't gone to that restaurant/bar/club/café, I would never have met you

You are my destiny

We are meant for each other
= *you're destined to be together*

Since I met you, I'm over the moon
= *over the moon means you're very happy*

You are my sun, my moon
and all my stars
E. E. Cummings

The moon, the stars, and you

It's a beautiful starry night

We've had a magical evening
= *magical means dreamy and wonderful*

You've cast a spell on me
= *he or she has attracted you as if by magic*

I'm bewitched by your charm
= *bewitched means you're attracted to someone, as if under a magic spell*

I'm under your spell
= *you're dazzled by his or her charm*

You are my Ms Right ♀
= *she's perfect for you*

You are my Prince Charming ♂
= *he's perfect for you*

Traditions of love: Lucky charms

Weddings are full of charms – things that are believed to bring the couple happiness and protect them from evil spirits in their future life together. In Britain you often see horseshoes at a wedding – now usually made of card or paper and covered in silver foil. Horseshoes have a smiling shape – if the right way up. A real horseshoe is often made of iron, and a long time ago iron was considered magical because of its strength and ability to withstand fire.

Of all the gin joints,
in all the towns, in all the world
she walks into mine
From the movie *Casablanca*

The past

A good catch is husband or wife material – someone who'd make a good husband and father or wife and mother

Have you ever been in love?

Who was your first love?

I broke up with my boyfriend/girlfriend *last year*
= the relationship is over

I'm separated
= you're married but no longer living with your husband or wife

I'm divorced

My wife/husband left me for someone else

She/he walked out on me
= she/he left the family home suddenly and without explanation

I'm a ♀ widow/♂ widower. My husband/wife passed away *three* years ago
= 'passed away' is a gentle way of saying someone has died

My ex-___ (ex = former)
— ex-boyfriend
— ex-girlfriend
— ex-husband
— ex-wife
— ex-partner

Has your heart been broken before?
— I was hurt before

I'm not ready for a relationship yet

I don't want to rush into a new relationship

I don't want to start a new relationship on the rebound
= *on the rebound means starting a new relationship just after
your old one has ended, because you're lonely*

I've had other boyfriends/girlfriends, but you are different

*If grass can grow through cement
love can find you
at every time in your life*
Cher

Heart and soul

I'm so happy when I'm with you

I think of you day and night

I want to be with you all the time

I feel a warm feeling inside whenever I'm with you

I'm crazy about you
= *crazy means madly in love*

Traditions of love: Diamonds

Diamonds may be a girl's best friend, but other gemstones can have magical powers, too. Turquoise is said to prevent arguments, and emerald to give success in love; red onyx is said to ensure a happy marriage, and topaz symbolizes fidelity or faithfulness.

Kiss me

You have a beautiful mouth
You have beautiful lips

Kiss me

A kiss is a lovely trick
designed by nature
to stop speech
when words become superfluous
Ingrid Bergman

Your lips are so soft
Your lips are so sweet

To steal a kiss
= *to kiss someone by surprise*

Blow me a kiss
= *if you blow someone a kiss, you kiss your fingers and blow the kiss to the person you love*

A peck on the cheek
= *a quick kiss on the side of your face*

Love bite
= *a bite on your neck from a lover*

French kiss
= *a French kiss is a lover's kiss, mouth to mouth*

Traditions of love: Kiss the bride

After the wedding ceremony, the husband and wife kiss each other

Body language (hugs and cuddles)

Hug
= *when someone puts their arms around you and squeezes*

Cuddle
= *a cuddle is a long hug with someone you love, for example on the sofa*

Snuggle
= *snuggle means to sit or lie close together, in body contact*

Smooch
= *to dance together slowly, with your arms around each other*

Embrace
= *to put your arms round someone you love*

Pinch
= *to nip someone playfully, especially on the bottom, with your finger and thumb*

Clingy
= *if your boyfriend or girlfriend is clingy, he or she sticks to you like glue, so much so that you feel uncomfortable*

Cold shoulder
= *if someone gives you the cold shoulder, they ignore you*

Traditions of love: Kissing under the mistletoe

Mistletoe is a small plant with white berries used as Yuletide decoration. In ancient Britain, druids collected the poisonous berries to make them into a potion against unfruitfulness. This theme of fertility survives in English-speaking countries today where, by tradition, couples kiss under the mistletoe at Christmas.

You must remember this
A kiss is just a kiss, a sigh is just a sigh
The fundamental things apply
As time goes by
From the movie *Casablanca*

Communication (speaking your language)

*There's no word in any language to describe
how beautiful you are*

*The most romantic way to learn a language is with someone
you love*

Can you speak English?

I'm not very good at English. Could you help me?

Will you teach me *your language*?
— If you teach me English

I'm sorry, I don't understand

I can't put it into words
= *it's difficult to express how you feel in words*

Your English is great!
— I love your accent

How do you say this in English?

How do you say ___ in *your language*?

How do you say 'I love you'?

If I could rearrange the alphabet
I'd put U and I together

Heart to heart (saying what you feel)

The best and most beautiful things in the world
cannot be seen or even touched
They must be felt with the heart
Helen Keller

I want to tell you how I feel

Don't hold back
= *tell me your true feelings*

I've never felt this way before

I can't stop thinking about you

You are___
— so kind and generous
— such a loving person
— just perfect

I love___
— your smile
— the way you laugh
— you

I fall in love with you every time I look into your eyes

You make me laugh
You make me happy

I can feel something special between us

Is this love?

Is this just a fling or something more serious?
= *a fling is a brief and casual relationship*

Are we just good friends, or something more?

Traditions of love: The heart

The heart is the symbol of love, and English has many expressions using the word 'heart'. Here are just a few...

Sweetheart
= *your sweetheart is the person you love*

Heart-throb ♂
= *a heart-throb is a famous man that women adore*

Heart on your sleeve
= *if you wear your heart on your sleeve, you show your emotions openly*

Heart in your mouth
= *if your heart is in your mouth, you are anxious about what's about to happen*

Change of heart
= *a change of heart means a change of mind*

Heart sinks
= *if your heart sinks, you are losing hope*

Lose heart
= *if you lose heart, you lose hope*

Broken heart
= *if you lose love, you say your heart is broken*

Warm-hearted
= *a warm-hearted person is kind and sympathetic*

Cold-hearted
= *a cold-hearted person is cruel and unfeeling*

Heartless
= *a heartless person is cruel and cold*

Hard-hearted
= *if you are hard-hearted, you have no feelings*

Down-hearted
= *if you are down-hearted, you are sad*

Half-hearted
= *if you do something half-heartedly, you do it without enthusiasm*

Heart-to-heart
= *very close between two people*

From the bottom of my heart
= *sincerely*

Traditions of love: Bridesmaids and pageboys

The bride and groom are often accompanied at their wedding by a small child or children – called bridesmaids and pageboys. The children symbolize the couple's future family.

Thinking things over

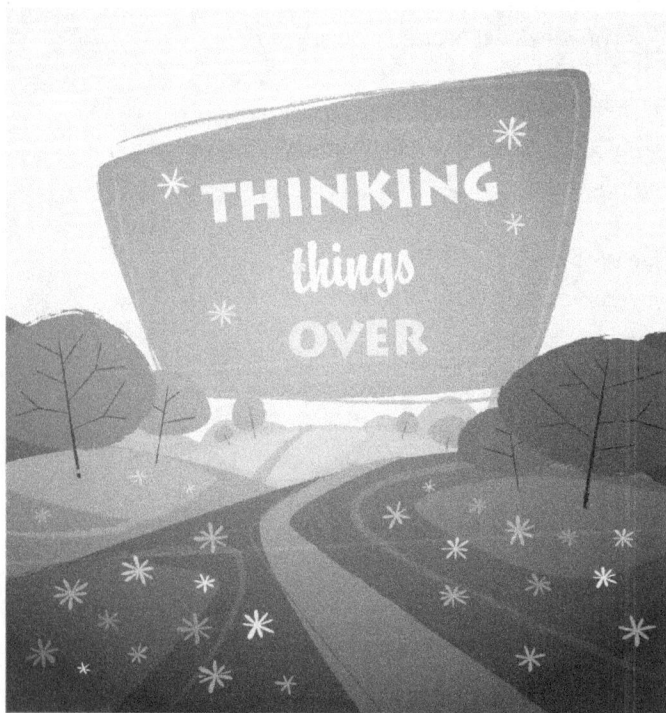

I need time to think

I like you a lot, but I need more time

I have a million thoughts in my head
= *you're uncertain*

You're a really wonderful person, but I need to be sure of my feelings

This has been such a whirlwind romance
= *a short, passionate romance that becomes serious very quickly*

I need to be sure that you love me

What's to come is still unsure
In delay there lies no plenty
Then come kiss me, sweet and twenty
Youth's a stuff will not endure
Shakespeare, *Twelfth Night*

Sweet nothings

Sugar, oh, honey, honey
You are my candy girl
The Archies

Sweet nothings are words of love and affection between lovers

In English, you can call your partner...

Something romantic...
Darling

Something sweet...
Sugar
Honey
Sweetheart
Sugar daddy ♂
= *an older man who showers a young woman with expensive gifts*

Like a baby...
Babe ♀
Baby ♀

Something heavenly...
Angel ♀

Traditions of love: Almonds and marzipan

Marzipan is a common ingredient in wedding cakes. It's a paste made of almonds, which are egg-shaped nuts symbolizing fertility. It is hoped that eating them will bless the couple with lots of children.

Valentines

Roses are red, violets are blue
Sugar is sweet, and so are you

Valentine is the saint of lovers, and Valentine's Day is celebrated on 14th February. It's a special day when people send a message or gift to the person they love.

Valentine's Day began with the Roman festival of Lupercalia, which celebrated the coming of spring. Valentine was a priest who was imprisoned by the Roman emperor. He fell in love with his jailer's daughter and wrote a letter to her before he died, signed 'from your Valentine'.

The oldest Valentine in English was written by Margery Brews to her fiancé John Paston in February 1477. Margery tells John she is not in good health 'of body, nor of herte'. Her mother had tried to persuade her father, unsuccessfully, to raise Margery's dowry – the money and valuables given by a bride to her husband upon marriage. Margery writes to John, 'if that ye loffe "love" me...ye will not leffe "leave" me'. There is a happy ending to the story, as John and Margery marry.

By tradition, young women thought the first man they saw on February 14th would be the one they would marry. So they avoided looking at the wrong man!

Today, lovers give cards and gifts such as chocolates and red roses. The customs of giving red roses began when the French king, Louis XVI, gave his queen, Marie Antoinette, red roses on Valentine's Day.

Sometimes senders, especially couples, sign their names, but often the sender of the Valentine is secret...

My funny valentine
Sweet comic valentine
You make me smile with my heart
Ella Fitzgerald

Lovey-dovey

To my Valentine
With all my love
X?

Lovey-dovey means sweetly romantic, like two doves cooing

Saying it with flowers

I'd like to ride my bicycle with you on the handlebars
Alessi Brothers, *O Lori*

Traditions of love: Flowers

Wedding flowers – the bride's bouquet, the groom's buttonhole or boutonniere, and the wedding reception adorned with blooms – symbolize beauty, love and abundance. Traditionally in England, young girls scattered flowers before the bride as she walked to church. Today in America, a flower girl walks in front of the bride with a basket of petals.

A message with flowers

To my darling Name
With love
Your name

Traditions of love: Throwing the bouquet

Before the bride leaves the wedding reception, she throws her bouquet over her shoulder. Whoever catches the bouquet will be the next to marry. Sometimes the bridegroom throws his buttonhole or boutonniere, too.

Our song

This song was playing when we met. Do you remember?

I love this song

I love the lyrics of this song
= *the words of a song*

When I hear this song, I think of us

If music be the food of love
play on
Shakespeare

Traditions of love: Bells, horns, fireworks and tin cans

At a church wedding bells are often rung and, as the bride and groom leave, guests often sound their car horns. The couple's friends also tie tin cans to the back of the wedding car, and there may be fireworks, too. All this noise is to scare away evil spirits from the happy couple.

Being apart

I can't wait to see you again
= *I want to see you soon*

I'll call you as soon as I get there

I'll call/Skype®/email/text every day

I'll wait forever and a day for you

It's wonderful to ___
— hear your voice
— hear your laugh
— see your face
— see your smile

I won't last a day without you
The Carpenters

I miss you

I'm lonely without you

I'm miserable without you

I cry myself to sleep when you're not here

It hurts when we are apart

I'm lovesick
= *you love someone so much your stomach aches and you cannot eat*

I can't stop thinking about you

Don't cry

Messages of love

Life without you is like a broken pencil: pointless
Anonymous

Texting and email

What are you doing now?
— I was thinking of you

I'll send you our pictures from today

I miss you

Goodnight

Sweet dreams

Love letters

You can start your letter, text or email with 'My darling'

I miss you

You're the first thing I think of when I wake up in the morning

I long to see you again
= *I want to see you again so much*

I long to kiss you again

You are my hero ♂

Your hair brushed against my skin and I could smell your perfume ♀

You are beyond compare
= you're the most wonderful person in the world

I want our love to last forever

At the end of your letter, xxx means three kisses

Love forever,
Name
xxx

Love letters straight from your heart
Keep us so near while apart
Nat King Cole

Romantic evenings at home

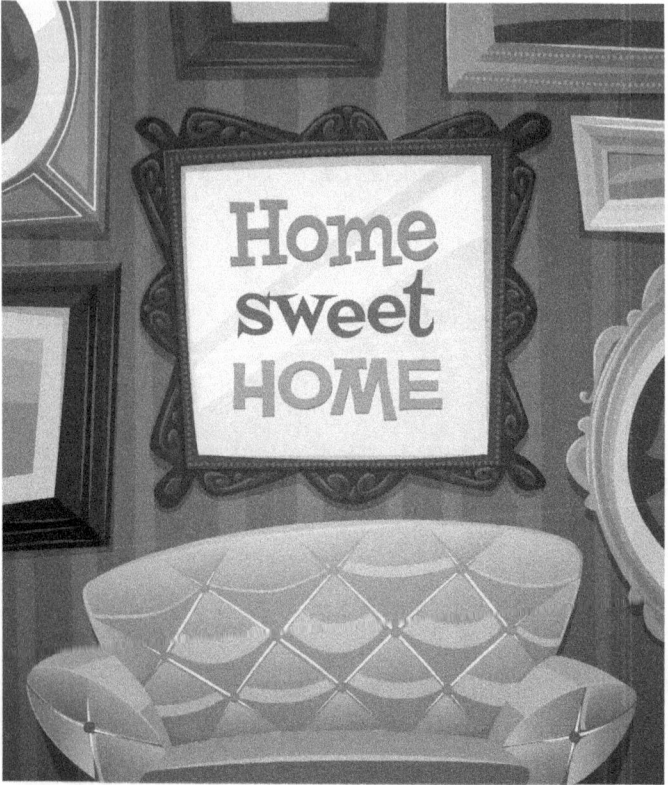

Shall we stay in tonight?
= *spend the evening at home together*

What time shall I come over?
= *what time shall I come to your place?*

Shall we watch a movie?
What would you like to watch?

Shall we cook *dinner* together?
What would you like to eat?

I'll cook something from *my country*

Do I love you because you're beautiful
Or are you beautiful because I love you?
Oscar Hammerstein

Try a little bite!
— What is it?

It's a special food/drink from *my country*

Do you like it?
— It's unusual

It's divine/delicious
= *divine means it tastes heavenly*

Would you like something sweet for dessert?

Traditions of love: A spoonful of love

In Wales men carved spoons out of wood for the woman they loved. The love spoons were decorated with hearts, keys and keyholes, so the woman could unlock the man's heart.

Still today in Britain, people often give a gift of a silver spoon to a newborn baby.

Love and affection

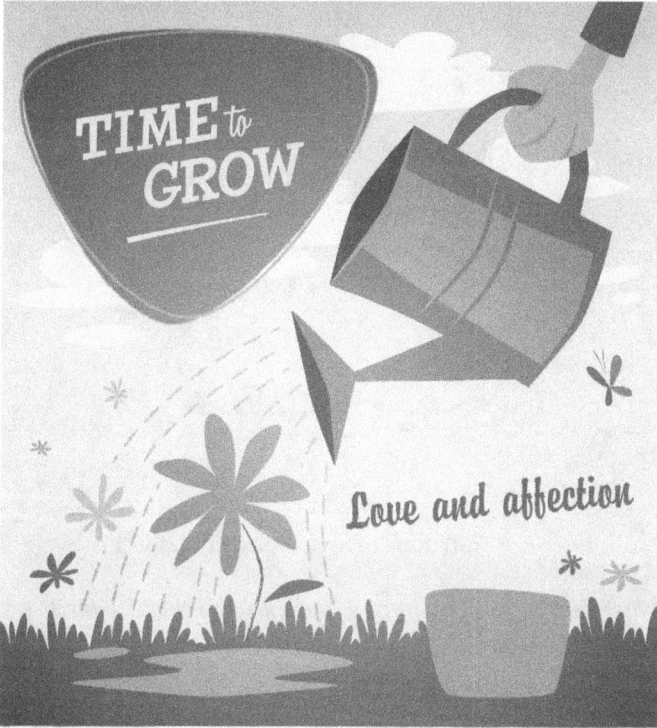

Hold my hand
— Hold me

Give me a hug
— Kiss me

I love you to bits

= *a funny way of saying you love him or her a lot*

This is the end of a beautiful friendship
I know for your eyes told me so...
That was the end of a beautiful friendship
And just the beginning of love
Nat King Cole

Traditions of love: Baby's breath

The plant baby's breath or gypsophila paniculata, with its puff of tiny white flowers, is a symbol of fertility. It is often added to a bride's wedding bouquet.

Romantic getaway

A romantic getaway is a short vacation together, such as a weekend away

Shall we go away this weekend?

Where would you like to go?

Where shall we stay?

What about a romantic hotel or B&B (= bed and breakfast, a small hotel) ___ ?

— by the sea
— in the mountains
— by a lake
— in the country
— in the city

A thousand kisses from you
is never enough
Luther Vandross

Traditions of love: Getting to the church

Until about a hundred years ago the bridal party usually walked to the church on foot. A bridal carriage – whether horse-drawn or a car – should never turn around at the church gate – it would be bad luck. When the couple leave for honeymoon, their car is often decorated with a sign saying 'Just Married'.

Sweet talk

I love your __
— smile
— eyes
— laugh
— dimples (= the small dents in your cheeks when you smile)
— tummy button (= your navel)
— bottom

I love your perfume ♀
I love your smell ♂
You smell heavenly

You look divine ♀
You're beautiful

You're irresistible
You're good enough to eat

*You make me melt
like hot fudge on a sundae*

Can you read my thoughts?

You're blushing
*= blushing is when your face goes red when you're
embarrassed*

Kiss me

Traditions of love: Myrtle

Myrtle, with its small egg-shaped leaves and white flowers, was a symbol of love in Greece and Rome. Traditionally in England, after a wedding a bridesmaid plants a sprig of myrtle from the bride's bouquet. When it flowers, there will be a new wedding.

Making love

Kiss me
— Hold me

Don't go
Stay with me tonight
— I don't want to go home tonight

I think of you day and night

You are beautiful
— You're very sexy

You're so hot
= hot means sexy

Your kisses make me tingle all over
= a tingle is a feeling of excitement, like electricity running down your body

I want to make love to you
— Make love to me

I'm nervous

Have you had many girlfriends/boyfriends?

It's my first time
— Mine, too

You have beautiful ___
— eyes
— skin
— hair
— hands

I love your ___
— smile
— mouth
— lips
— nose
— dimples (= the small dents in your cheeks when you smile)

Your skin is so soft

The voice of your eyes is deeper than all roses
Nobody, not even the rain, has such small hands
E. E. Cummings

I love your ___
— perfume ♀
— cologne ♂

You smell wonderful

I love your curves ♀
= *your curvy figure*

You have a beautiful ___
— figure
— tummy (= stomach)
— back
— bottom

I want to kiss you all over

I love it when you do that
I don't like it when you do that

*Of all the beautiful curves on your body
your smile is my favorite*
Anonymous

I love your caress
= *caress means to stroke someone tenderly*

Touch me here

That feels divine *or* heavenly

I'm tingling all over

Are you hungry?
— I want to eat you up

I want you

Love me do
The Beatles

Him

Eyes
Lips
Mouth
Smile
Ear lobe (= the soft bottom part of his ear)
Stubble (= the short hair on his face)
Neck
Shoulders
Arms

Hands
Chest
Stomach
Hair
Tummy button
Back
Bottom
Thigh (= the top part of his leg)
Legs
Feet
Toes

Her

Eyes
Eye lashes
Lips
Mouth
Smile
Ear lobe (= the soft bottom part of her ear)
Hair
Neck
The nape of your neck (= the back of her neck)
Breast
Tummy button

Stomach
Back
Waist
Hips
Bottom
Thigh (= the top part of her leg)
Legs
Feet
Toes

Traditions of love: The wedding bed

Knots symbolize infertility – so traditionally in Scotland the bride and groom loosened every knot of their clothing.

In rural England, the bridal suite was arranged so that the harvest moon would shine on the wedding bed, helping the couple conceive a child.

Saying no

I don't want to

I'm not ready

I'm tired

The time isn't right
I want to wait until the time is right

♀ It's not safe now
♀ I'm having my period

I don't want to just sleep around
= *sleep around means to have many partners*

No!

Leave me alone!
= *don't touch me*

Go away!

Pillow talk

Pillow talk means a conversation in bed

Hold me tight

I love you

That was heavenly

That was divine
= divine means heavenly

That was sheer bliss
= sheer bliss means perfect happiness

You were wonderful

You were as sweet as cherry pie
Wild as Friday night
Sade

You were so ___
— sweet
— tender
— gentle
— affectionate

You are so passionate

I've never felt like that before

You're very masculine ♂
You're very feminine ♀

I love watching you while are sleeping

Stay with me forever

Breakfast in bed

Would you like some breakfast?

Would you like breakfast in bed?

Would you like some ___?
__ tea
__ coffee
__ orange juice
__ toast
__ eggs

Traditions of love: The wedding breakfast

The wedding breakfast is the meal served after the wedding ceremony, regardless of the time of day. The bride, groom and wedding guests share in eating and drinking together, symbolizing the union of the couple, their families and friends.

How d'ya like your eggs in the morning?
I like mine with a kiss
Dean Martin and Helen O'Connell

Lovers' tiffs (working it out)

A tiff is a small quarrel

What's wrong

What's the matter?

Did I do something wrong?

Please tell me

Is it me?
= *is it something I've said or done?*

I don't like it when you ___
— ignore me
— stop talking
— get upset
— shout

It really hurts me when you ___
— do that
— say that

I'm tired of your behavior

I'm really angry with you
— Why are you angry with me?

I'm angry because you ___
— didn't call
— were late

Communication

Don't say that

We need to talk

You never want to talk
— Why won't you talk to me?

You never listen to me
— You never listen to what I say

You interrupt me when I'm talking
— Please let me finish

You always ignore me
— I feel like I'm invisible

You never tell me how you feel
You never tell me you love me

It doesn't matter
— It does matter

Why didn't you call me?

Why didn't you reply to my messages
= messages can mean voicemail, email or text

You left without saying anything
You left in a huff
= in an angry mood

I didn't hear anything from you *for hours/days/weeks*

I tried to call you, but ___
— you didn't answer
— I was busy

I tried to talk to you many times, but I couldn't

The course of true love never did run smooth
Shakespeare

Misunderstanding

I don't understand

I'm confused

What do you mean?

I can't understand why ___

Please try to understand my feelings

I'm sorry. I misunderstood you

Uncertainty

I don't know what to do

You said you love me

I'm not sure if I love you

I'm afraid that you will leave me

Stood up

Stood up means you arranged a date with him or her, but they didn't come

Why didn't you come?

I waited *two* hours for you

Why didn't you call?
Why didn't you answer?

I tried to call/email/text you

I was busy
I couldn't get away from work

Something came up
= *an unexpected event prevented you from contacting him or her*

Character

You are __
— arrogant
— so bitter
— bossy
— cruel
— cynical (= you believe the worst about people)
— always finding fault (= you find faults in everything)
— a fool with money
— full of yourself (= you think you're great)
— heartless (= you have no feelings for others)
— impatient
— inconsiderate (= you don't consider other's feelings)
— insensitive (= you don't notice other people's feelings)
— jealous
— lazy
— mean
— moody
— always nagging me (= he or she criticizes you constantly)
— negative about everything
— nit-picking (= you find small faults in everything)
— oversensitive (= you're too sensitive)
— too possessive (= you want to control his or her life)
— quick-tempered (= you lose your temper easily)
— rude
— self-centered (= you only think of yourself)
— a slob (= you're lazy and slovenly)
— stubborn

— unreliable
— vain

You act like a child
Grow up!

Love will find a way
Proverb

Honesty

I don't believe you

Please tell me the truth

You're lying
Don't lie

You deceived me

Look me in the eye
= *look into my eyes so I can know if you're telling the truth*

Trust

I don't trust you

You've betrayed my trust

I've lost all trust in you

How can I ever trust you again?

A woman knows very well that, though a wit sends her his poems, praises her judgment, solicits her criticism, and drinks her tea, this by no means signifies that he respects her opinions
Virginia Woolf

Promise

Promise me that you will always ___

Promise me that you will never ___

Don't break your promise

Acceptance

Why are you trying to change me?

Can't you accept me for who I am?

Equality

I give and you take
= *you give everything in the relationship but receive little in return*

You always put me down
= *he or she insults and humiliates you*

You humiliate me in front of your friends

You treat me like a doormat
= *a doormat is a mat on which you wipe your shoes*

Nothing I do is ever good enough

Love and affection

You never show me any affection

It feels like you don't care

You're so cold towards me

I want to feel close to you

The blame game

Please don't blame me

It's not my fault
It's your fault

It's both our faults

Feeling blue

I feel empty inside
I feel so small

I'm worried
— What about?

I've been crying my heart out
= *you've been crying for hours*

Do you want to talk about it?

Stay with me

Don't leave me tonight

Don't worry, I'm here with you

Do you want a shoulder to cry on?
= *a shoulder to cry on is someone to console you when you're feeling blue*

One word frees us
Of all the weight and pain in life
That word is Love
Socrates

You're always someone I can turn to
= *you're always there for him or her*

Would you like a hot bath?

I can make you dinner

Cheer me up
= *please do something to make me feel better*

I want to make you happy

We can get through this together

Broken heart

Nothing compares to you
Sinead O'Connor

I want to break up
= *to end the relationship*

I want to separate
= *to break up, perhaps for a while, perhaps forever*

It's over
= *the relationship has no future*

I'm leaving

Why?

We're too different

I need some space
= *you need to be apart from him or her*

I need some time
= *you need time to think*

I want to meet other people
= *you want to try to find a new partner*

I've met someone else

Intimacy

Don't you love me?

I want to feel loved

I feel starved of affection

You never show your feelings

You're so cold towards me

You've got a heart of stone
= *your heart is cold and hard*

You don't care about my feelings

You take me for granted
= *he or she doesn't value you*

You treat me like I'm part of the furniture
= *he or she treats you like an object rather than someone they love*

You never show any appreciation for anything I do

I'm fed up
= *you're tired of this relationship*

We are drifting apart
= *you're slowly moving apart*

The spark has gone from our relationship
= *your relationship is dull and no longer exciting*

The passion has gone

We are like brother and sister
= *you love each other, but your relationship is not sexual*

We've fallen out of love
= *the opposite of falling in love. It means you no longer love someone*

I need more

I want more from a relationship

I'm bored with our relationship

I'm like you a lot, but that's not enough

I'm very fond of you, but I don't love you

I don't love you anymore

I don't think you love me anymore

You're too good for me
= *your partner is a good person and/or attractive, but you are not*

*Never allow someone to be your priority
while allowing yourself to be their option*
Mark Twain

Whither?

Where is our relationship going?

I want it to lead to something

Commitment

We never talk about our future

I need more commitment

Are you afraid to commit?
= *you're afraid to marry someone*

You have commitment phobia
= *you have a fear of marriage*

Why won't you marry me?

I don't want to be tied down
= *you don't want to lose your freedom*

I'm not ready to settle down
= *settle down means get married*

Compatibility

We're too different

We've nothing in common

We're not compatible

You've changed

Each night I put my head to my pillow
I try to tell myself I'm strong
because I've gone one more day without you
Anonymous

Someone else

Are you in love with someone else?

I saw you with another guy/girl/man/woman

I saw you flirting with that guy/girl/man/woman

I've seen you making eyes at other guys/girls/men/women
= *to invite someone with your eyes*

Have you been seeing someone behind my back?
= *seeing someone in secret*

Have you been cheating on me?
= *cheating means having a relationship with someone else*

Are you having an affair?
= *an affair is when a husband or wife has another lover*

Tell me the truth
Please don't lie

There's no one else
I haven't met anyone else

I only have eyes for you
= *you never look at anyone else*

I've met someone else. I'm so sorry

I've fallen in love with someone else
— That explains everything

I didn't mean to hurt you
— You didn't care about me

I hate myself

I was so naïve to trust you
How could you do that?

You are a lying cheat

I'm all mixed up inside
= you're not sure who you love

Fault

It's all your fault

You've ruined everything
You've ruined my life

Don't blame me

Don't blame yourself
It's not your fault

You're not to blame

It's all my fault

'Tis better to have loved and lost
Than never to have loved at all
Tennyson

Understanding

Thank you for telling me

I appreciate your honesty

I understand

Just good friends

Can we still be friends?

Can we keep in touch?

Never forget

I'll never forget you

I'll never forget the times we had together

Please don't forget me

I'll cherish every moment we had together

I'll always treasure the time we had together

Don't go

Please go
I have to go

Please don't go
Please don't leave me

Don't leave me like this

I need you
I don't want to lose you

I can't bear to be without you

I'll never find someone like you

I gave you everything

I still love you
I will always love you

I feel completely alone

The end

Is this the end?

Do you want to break up?

It's over

I made a big mistake

I never want to see you again

I wish I never had met you

Let's not end like this

You've broken my heart
= *a broken heart means the pain of losing your love*

I gave you my heart and soul
= *you gave them your love, your body, everything*

I don't know if I can ever forgive you

It's too late

It's hopeless

I can't take any more
I can't go on like this

I'm leaving

I love you
I hate you

*There is nothing more beautiful
than a person whose heart has been broken
but still believes in love*
Anonymous

Making up

Making up means getting together again after an argument or breakup

You pierce my soul. I am half agony, half hope.
Tell me not that I am too late,
that such precious feelings are gone for ever.
I offer myself to you again with a heart even more your own
than when you almost broke it ...
Dare not say that man forgets sooner than woman,
that his love has an earlier death.
I have loved none but you.
Jane Austen, *Persuasion*

Talking it over

Do you want to talk about it?

Please call me

Let's not fall out over something like this
= *fall out means you're no longer friends*

We're just going through a bad patch
= *a bad patch is a difficult period in a relationship*

I miss you so much

I cry myself to sleep

I'm hurting inside

I'm lonely without you

I'm lost without you
= *without him or her, you can't find your way in life*

Without you my life is empty

Three little words

Three little words means 'I LOVE YOU'

We were so happy

We were so good together
= *you had a great relationship*

I love you so much

You're the best thing that ever happened to me
= *you made his or her life wonderful*

No one can replace you

Morning without you
is a dwindled dawn
Emily Dickinson

Consoling

Console means to comfort someone when they are sad

Please don't cry

Don't be upset

Let me wipe your tears

We can work it out

Let's try again

We can work it out

Can we get back together?

I'm such a fool

I can change

Actions speak louder than words
= *he or she must show that they mean what they say by their actions*

Can you forgive me?

Can you give me a second chance?

Respect

Please show me some respect

Don't lose your temper with me

Don't shout at me

Don't behave like that. It demeans you
= *his or her behavior is unworthy of them*

You're my best friend as well as my
boyfriend/girlfriend/husband/wife, so please respect me

I don't want to be treated this way

How would you feel if I treated you the way you treat me?

What would you do in my shoes?
= *what would you do if you were me?*

You never listen to me

You never let me finish what I'm going to say

Don't change the subject
= *when he or she starts talking about something else rather
than discussing what's wrong*

Don't talk down to me
= *talk down means he or she talks to you as if you were
inferior*

Don't mansplain everything to me
= *when a man explains something to a woman in a patronizing
manner*

Don't tell me what to do

You're always criticizing me. Do you think *you* are perfect?

You never think about my feelings

I need to feel appreciated

You always take me for granted
= *he or she doesn't value you*

You're just using me
= *he or she is only interested in you for sex*

Don't hurt me any more

I've lost all respect for you

The beauty of a woman must be seen from in her eyes
Because that is the doorway to her heart
The place where love resides
Audrey Hepburn

Putting it right

What's the matter?

Are you OK?

Do you want to talk about it?

Please tell me what's on your mind

I'm listening

I want to talk about it

Let's talk it over
= *let's try to fix this problem together*

How was your day?
How was work?

— I'm really stressed
— I'm just tired

I'm feeling a little down
I think I'm coming down with a cold

Tell me what happened
I want to know
Please share it with me

I understand
I understand how you feel

— You're a good listener

Thanks for all your help today. I really appreciate it

I'm so proud of you

You are a wonderful man/woman

Hold me

Give me a hug

I respect you

I love you

Saying sorry

I've fallen in love many times
Always with you
Anonymous

I'm so sorry
— I'm sorry too

I'm sorry I ___
— said that
— did that

It's all my fault

I was wrong
You were right

I made a stupid mistake

I didn't mean what I said

I didn't mean to upset you

I love you

I never want to leave you

The power of love

Omnia vincit amor
Love conquers all

Virgil 70–19 BCE

I loved you from the moment I saw you

Meeting you has been like a dream

We've had the time of our lives
= *the most wonderful time of your lives*

In you I have found someone I love to be with

Is this just a fling or something more serious?
= *a fling is a casual relationship that only lasts a short time*

The One

You're the One

From the moment I saw you, I knew you were the One
= *the One is the person you want to spend the rest of your life with*

The love of your life

You are the love of my life
= *the person you will love all your life*

You're the most important person in my life

You mean everything to me

I love you

I didn't know it was possible to love someone as much as I love you

I don't want this to end

Love is patient, love is kind.
It does not envy, it does not boast, it is not proud.
It does not dishonor others, it is not self-seeking,
it is not easily angered, it keeps no record of wrongs.
Love does not delight in evil but rejoices with the truth.
It always protects, always trusts, always hopes, always perseveres.
Love never fails.
Corinthians

Getting engaged (proposals)

*When you realize you want to spend
the rest of your life with somebody,
you want the rest of your life
to start as soon as possible*
When Harry Met Sally

At the right romantic moment...

We've been dating for a *year/three years* now

Hold my hand

I've never felt like this before
I dream of our future together

I want to share my life with you
I want to spend the rest of my life with you

Be mine forever

Do you feel the same?

My heart is in your hands
= *your happiness depends on his or her answer*

Proposing

Will you marry me?
The traditional way for men to propose is to get down on one knee and ask 'Will you marry me?'

Popping the question
'Pop' means to ask; the question is 'Will you marry me?'

Yes!
I love you

I feel a little giddy
= *giddy means dizzy with excitement*

Let's call our families

Save the date
= *save the date means your family and friends should enter the date of your wedding in their calendars*

Traditions of love: Leap year

In a leap year, by tradition women propose to men

Diamonds are a girl's best friend
Marilyn Monroe

Getting engaged

Shall we get engaged?

Let's get engaged on *New Year's Eve/your birthday*
Let's get engaged in *London/New York*

Shall we choose a ring?

Do you like diamonds?

Husband and wife to-be

Fiancé ♂
= *the man you're engaged to*

Fiancée ♀
= *the woman you're engaged to*

Husband-to-be
= *your future husband*

Wife-to-be
= *your future wife*

Traditions of love: The ring

It's thought that the Romans started the custom of betrothal rings, symbolizing the promise of marriage. The ring's circular shape symbolizes endless love and fidelity. In the eighteenth and nineteenth centuries, rings with lapis lazuli, opal, verd antique, emerald, moonstone and epidote were popular. Their initials spell 'L-O-V-E M-E'.

Engagement and wedding rings are worn on the fourth finger of the left hand, because it was believed that a vein from that finger led direct to the heart.

Wedding dress

Until the 1800s, a poor bride didn't wear a special wedding dress – just her best dress. And the bridesmaids and groom's friends dressed like the wedding couple to confuse evil wishers.

Today, a bride usually wears a white wedding dress, but this custom is quite new – it became popular when Queen Victoria married in white in 1840.

Traditions of love: Old, new, borrowed and blue

Brides in English-speaking countries often wear something old, something new, something borrowed and something blue.

Bachelor party or Stag night

A stag, bachelor or buck's party is a party for the groom and his male friends before the wedding. A stag or buck is a male deer.

The party is a symbolic farewell to bachelorhood – a rite of passage before the groom enters married life.

Until a few hundred years ago, family and friends of the bride and groom would brew a special wedding beer, which they sold to raise money for the couple's new life. This was called 'bride ale' – and 'bridal' came to mean a wedding or wedding feast.

Today, many grooms have a stag weekend. Organized by the best man, friends often play a trick on the groom-to-be, such as putting him on a bus or train for some far-off destination.

Traditions of love: Wedding races

Traditionally a wedding race was held from the church to the bride's house. The prize was often the bride's garter, a lucky charm.

Hen night or Bachelorette party

A hen night is a party for the bride and her female friends before the wedding. Like the stag night or bachelor party, it is a rite of passage before the bride enters married life.

The party may be in fancy dress, and in Britain the bride-to-be may wear 'L-plates' – a sign with a large 'L' meaning 'Learner'.

Bridal shower and Honey-do

Offering gifts or money to the bride and groom is an important part of a wedding ceremony. In English-speaking countries, guests usually give something for the home. Sharp or pointed gifts are avoided as they could 'cut' the marriage.

In the past, a young woman would have a trousseau, French for 'little bundle', in which she collected linen, crockery and cutlery for her future married life. Today, this is called a 'hope chest' or 'bottom drawer'.

Another tradition is the 'bridewain', which was a decorated cart or wagon on which furniture and provisions were collected for the wedding couple.

In the USA, Canada, Australia and New Zealand today, female friends of the bride-to-be give her small gifts at a party called a 'bridal shower'. In Victorian times, the bride's friends placed small presents in Japanese paper parasols that, when opened, literally showered the bride with gifts.

A groom may also have a wedding shower, where he receives tools for working on the home. This is called a 'honey-do' shower, as after the wedding his wife can say 'Honey do this, honey do that' to make sure he does his share of household chores.

Getting married (saying I do)

Wedding plans

Bride ♀
= *the woman who is getting married*

Groom ♂ or bridegroom ♂
= *the man who is getting married*

To tie the knot
= *to get married*

Settle down
= *to marry and have a family*

Shall we have a wedding in *your country* or *my country*?

Shall we set a date?
= *set a date means to decide the date of your wedding*

Wedding invitations
= *cards sent to wedding guests, inviting them to your wedding*

Church wedding
= *a traditional wedding in church*

Civil ceremony
= *a wedding ceremony that's not religious*

A white wedding
= *a traditional wedding, in which the bride wears a white dress*

Chief bridesmaid or matron or maid of honor
= *the chief bridesmaid or matron or maid of honor looks after the bride at the wedding and takes care of the bridesmaids and pageboys*

Bridesmaid
= *a girl or woman who accompanies the bride at the wedding ceremony; bridesmaids are usually family members or friends*

Pageboy
= *a boy who accompanies the bride at the wedding*

Best man
= *the groom usually choses his best friend to be best man. It is a great honor. The best man helps the groom at his wedding: he gets the groom to the ceremony on time, and safeguards the ring until the groom places it on the bride's finger. The best man usually gives a speech at the wedding reception, reading messages of congratulation and telling stories about the groom's life.*

Usher
= *the ushers help the best man and show the wedding guests to their seats at the wedding ceremony*

I do, I do, I do, I do, I do
Abba

Wedding day

It is traditional for bride to arrive at the church after the groom

You look beautiful ♀

You look very handsome ♂

This is the happiest day of my life

The Big Day
= *your wedding day*

To walk down the aisle
= *get married; the aisle is the path in the middle of a church that leads up to the altar, where the bride and groom are married*

Given away
= *by tradition, a bride is 'given away' by her father. This means that he accompanies his daughter, arm in arm, down the aisle to her husband-to-be*

Veil
= the transparent material covering the bride's face

Wedding vows
= the solemn promises that the bride and groom make to each other at the wedding ceremony

Witness
= the witnesses are friends or family members of the couple who formally witness the marriage

Married name
= your family name after you get married

Maiden name ♀
= your family name before you were married

Jane Smith, née ♀ Jones
née is the French word for 'born'; it shows a woman's family name before she married, if she decided to change her name

Wedding bells
= the bells rung at a traditional church wedding

Wedding reception
= the meal and party to celebrate the marriage

Marquee
= sometimes a wedding reception is held in a large white tent, called a marquee

Toast
= *when all the wedding guests wish the bride and groom future happiness by drinking together*

Speeches
= *a wedding usually has several speeches – for instance, by the best man, the maid of honor, the groom, and the bride*

All you need is love
The Beatles

Traditions of love: Throwing rice

Wedding guests often throw rice over the bride and groom as they leave the church or other place of marriage. This old custom is to bless the couple with fertility by showering them with grain.

Similarly, confetti are small pieces of paper that guests throw over the bride and groom. Confetti comes from the Italian word 'confetto'. A confetto or comfit is a sugar-coated sweet contain-ing a nut or seed. Like rice, it's a fertility symbol to bless the couple with children.

Traditions of love: The wedding night

Traditionally in England the bride was put to bed by her brides-maids and the groom by his friends. The wedding party then joined in 'flinging the stocking': the groom's friends seized the bride's stockings, and the bridesmaids the groom's. They threw the stockings over their shoulders, and whoever they landed on would be the next to marry. Today, this tradition survives in throwing the bouquet.

Honeymoon

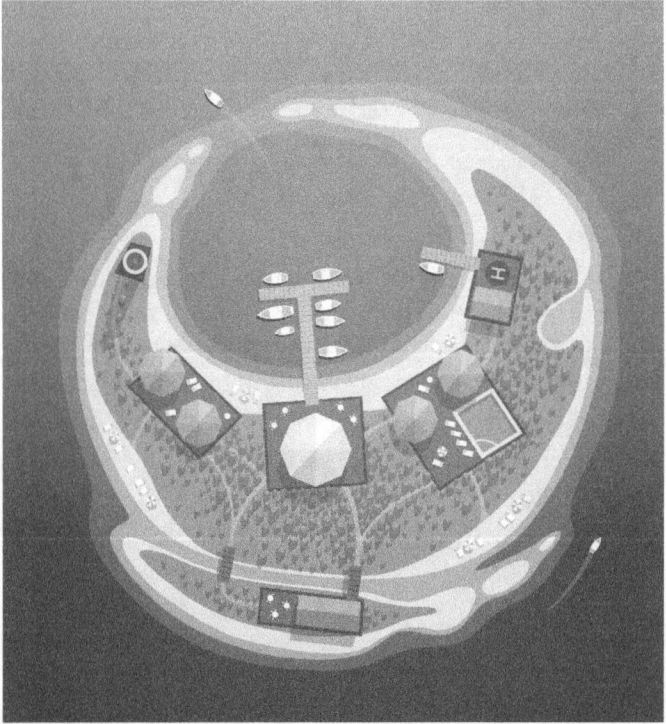

Fly me to the moon and let me dance among the stars
Frank Sinatra

No one knows the origin of the word 'honeymoon': 'honey' means sweetness, and 'moon' means months'. So 'honeymoon' probably symbolizes the sweet and sensual feelings of love after

*getting married. The honeymoon destination is often kept se-
cret by the couple.*

Newlyweds means a newly married couple

Where shall we go on honeymoon?
— Anywhere with you will be my dream come true

Shall we ___
— do some sightseeing?
— lie on the beach?
— stay in?
— order room service?
— have breakfast in bed?

Living together

Shall we move in together?

Would you like to move in with me?

Partner
= a partner is someone you live with as if husband or wife

This is my partner, Sam

Give and take

Give and take means learning to live with and respect someone else

I'm tired of your mess

You are really untidy

You leave things everywhere

Home is where the heart is
Proverb

I can't relax. You're always cleaning

You are really house-proud
= *someone who makes the house so tidy you can't relax*

I do everything. Please help me with the housework

You never lift a finger
= *you never help me*

I wait on you hand and foot
= *you're like a waitress or waiter to him or her*

You never have time for me. You're always working

I want to do things together

Traditions of love: Over the threshold

By tradition a husband carries his new bride over the threshold of their home, an old custom perhaps to protect her from evil spirits.

Having a baby

I want to have a baby with you

Shall we try for a baby?

I would like to hear the pitter-patter of tiny feet
= *you'd like to hear the pitter-patter sound of a toddler walking*

I look into your eyes and see our baby

I can see our baby in the twinkle in your eye
= *the look of love in your husband's eye before making a baby*

*Where there is love
there is life*
Mahatma Gandhi

Expecting

When you're expecting, it means you're pregnant

I'm pregnant
I think I'm pregnant

We're going to have a baby
We're going to be a family

That's wonderful!
I am so happy

You look radiant
= *a woman's healthy glow when she's expecting a baby*

Let's call our families!

Boy or girl

I'd love a boy *or* girl

We're expecting a boy/girl

We're expecting twins!

Let's choose a name

Birth

When is the baby due?
= *the date your baby will be born*

The baby's due in *Month*

The baby was 8lb 4oz

She/he was born on *date*

Baby traditions: Silver

Traditionally, gifts for a new baby were an egg, silver and salt, symbolizing fertility, wealth, and protecting from witchcraft. Still today, a common gift for a new baby is something made of silver.

Baby traditions: Blessing

After a baby is born, he or she is usually blessed in a special ceremony.

The father and his male friends often also celebrate the birth by sharing a drink to toast the mother and baby's health. This is called 'wetting the baby's head'.

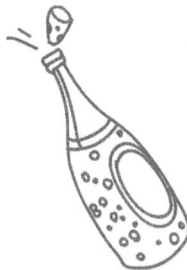

Anniversaries

It's our anniversary
It's *three* months/years since we met

It's our wedding anniversary
We got married *five* years ago

I love you with all my heart

To my darling husband/wife
Love forever
Your name

Traditions of love: Anniversaries

The bride and groom make a lifelong commitment to one another. Each wedding anniversary has a different celebration. The most common are:

1st paper
?nd cotton
3rd leather
4th silk
5th wood
10th tin
25th silver
50th gold

Soul mate

Your soul mate is the person you open your heart to with deep love, friendship and trust

*Love is composed of a single soul
inhabiting two bodies*
Aristotle

Happy ever after

Will you still need me, will you still feed me
When I'm sixty-four?
The Beatles

A marriage made in heaven

Ours is a marriage made in heaven
= *a perfect marriage*

Shall we tell our children our story one day?

Love me forever

And when two lovers woo
They still say 'I love you'
On that you can rely
No matter what the future brings
As time goes by
From the movie Casablanca

Credits

Author: Stephen Howe

Illustrations: Doremi and Primiaou/Shutterstock

Baker, Margaret (1974) *Folklore and Customs of Rural England*, London: David and Charles/New Jersey: Rowman and Littlefield.

Baker, Margaret (1977) *Wedding Customs and Folklore*, London: David and Charles/New Jersey: Rowman and Littlefield.

Briggs, Gill (2014) *Miraculous Mistletoe*, blog, Royal Horticultural Society: www.rhs.org.uk.

Encyclopædia Britannica Ultimate Reference Suite (2013) 'Cupid', 'Marriage', 'Myrtle', 'Ring', 'Valentine's Day', Chicago: Encyclopædia Britannica.

Monger, George P. (2013) *Marriage Customs of the World*, 2nd edition, Santa Barbara/Denver/Oxford: ABC-CLIO.

Montemurro, Beth (2006) *Something Old, Something Bold: Bridal Showers and Bachelorette Parties*, New Brunswick: Rutgers University Press.

Wilson, Carol (2005) 'Wedding Cake: A Slice of History', *Gastronomica* 5:2.

The End

www.ingramcontent.com/pod-product-compliance
Lightning Source LLC
La Vergne TN
LVHW051555080426
835510LV00020B/2984